THE ROYAL FAMILY

(A Fascinating Book Containing Royal Family Facts, Trivia, Images & Memory Recall Quiz: Suitable for Adults & Children)

Image Courtesy of Anonymous

For legal reasons we are obliged to state the following:

Copyright 2014 Matthew Harper

ISBN-13: 978-1499269819

ISBN-10: 1499269811

All rights reserved. No reproduction, copying or transmission of this publication, CD's or DVD included in this system may be made without written permission. No paragraph of this publication may be reproduced, copied or transmitted without written permission, or in accordance with the Copyright Act 1956 (amended).

Hi and a very warm welcome to "The Royal Family".

I'm one of those people who loves to hear about extraordinary facts or trivia about anything. They seem to be one of the few things my memory can actually recall. I'm not sure if it's to do with the shock or the "WoW" factor but for some reason my brain seems to store at least some of it for a later date.

I've always been a great believer in that whatever the subject, if a good teacher can inspire you and hold your attention, then you'll learn! Now I'm not a teacher but the system I've used in previous publications on Amazon seems to work well, particularly with children.

This edition includes a selection of those "WoW" facts combined with some pretty awesome pictures, if I say so myself! At the end there is a short "True or False" quiz to check memory recall and to help cement some of the information included in the book. Don't worry though, it's a bit of fun but at the same time, it helps to check your understanding.

Please note that if you're an expert on this particular subject then you may not find anything new here. If however you enjoy hearing sensational and extraordinary trivia and you like looking at some great pictures then I think you'll love it.

Matt.

I thought that before we get down to some of those amazing facts about the "Royal Family", we might begin with some snapshots, just to get the juices flowing……….

Queen Elizabeth II

Image Courtesy of Michael Gwyther-Jones

Prince Philip

Prince Charles

Princess Anne

Image Courtesy of Graham Grinner Lewis

Prince Andrew

Image Courtesy of Roosewelt Pinheiro/ABr

Prince Edward

Image Courtesy of Surtsicna

Sophie, Countess of Wessex

Image Courtesy of Frankie Fouganthin

Prince William

Image Courtesy of Gridge

Catherine, Duchess of Cambridge

Image Courtesy of Surtsicna

Prince Harry

Image Courtesy of Surtsicna

Okay, that's it for the warm up, let's get on with the game......

Image Courtesy of mr_johnnyp

Did you know that it was Queen Victoria who reigned from 1837 to 1901? She is the longest reigning British monarch in history so far!

Did you know that Prince Philip celebrated not one but two stag nights before his wedding to Queen Elizabeth II?

Image Courtesy of BiblioArchives LibraryArchives

Did you know that the wedding dress used by Elizabeth II was designed by Sir Norman Hartnell?

Image Courtesy of City of Allan warren

Did you know that Prince William's full name is William Arthur Philip Louis of Wales?

Image Courtesy of hapinachu

Did you know that Princess Diana's wedding dress was designed by David Emanuel and his wife Elizabeth?

Did you know that St James's Palace is the royal house of both Princes William and Harry?

Image Courtesy of ChrisO

Did you know that Queen Elizabeth described the year 1992 as her '*Annus horribilis*' due to the various negative family occurrences?

Bundesarchiv, Bild 199-1992-089-19A / CC-BY-SA

Did you know that out of respect for Princess Diana, Camilla does not use the title of the Princess of Wales even though it's her official title?

Image Courtesy of John C Williams

Did you know that in 1917, George V changed the family title of Saxe-Coburg-Gotha to Windsor due to the anti-German feeling at the time?

Did you also know that George V had a tattoo of a dragon on his right arm after he visited Japan?

XAM NGHE THUAT NGUYEN TATTOO

Did you know that Queen Victoria was actually born Princess Alexandrina of Kent?

Princess Victoria Aged 4

Did you know that Queen Elizabeth's official residence in Scotland is called the Palace of Holyroodhouse which is located in Edinburgh?

Image Courtesy of Pip R. Lagenta

Did you know that Prince Charles is heavily rumoured to take the title of George VII if he takes the throne?

Image Courtesy of Karen Roe

Did you know that Queen Elizabeth II is assumed to have sent over 40,000 Christmas cards during her reign as monarch?

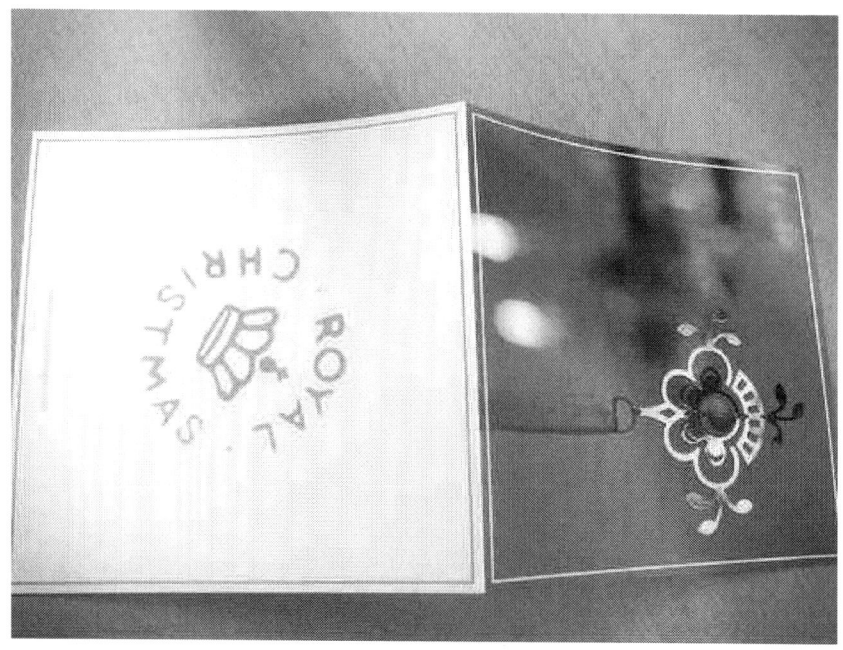

Image Courtesy of jacobms

Did you know that no monarch of England has yet held a university degree?

Image Courtesy of Tavin

Did you know that Prince Philip and Elizabeth II share the same grandmother, Queen Victoria?

Did you know that next five princes in line of succession to the throne are Prince Charles, Prince William, then his son Prince George, Prince Harry and then Prince Andrew?

Image Courtesy of Carfax2

Did you know that Lady Louise Windsor is the only daughter of Prince Edward and Sophie?

Image Courtesy of Surtsicna

Did you know that the first female next in line to the throne is Princess Beatrice the daughter of Prince Andrew and Sarah?

Image Courtesy of TheMatthewSlack

Did you know that Prince Harry was actually born Prince Henry of Wales?

Image Courtesy of Keith Laverack

Did you know that during World War II, Queen Elizabeth operated as part of the Auxiliary Territorial Service where she took part in a driving course?

Did you know that Prince Andrew's golf handicap qualifies him to play at a professional level?

Image Courtesy of Carfax2

Did you know that Queen Elizabeth introduced the dorgi which is a cross between a corgi and a dachshund?

Image Courtesy of ozmafan

Did you know that Prince William and Kate decided not to have servants in their home, a break in royal tradition?

Image Courtesy of UK_repsome

Did you know that the Queen of England's official title is the Queen of the United Kingdom of Great Britain and Northern Ireland?

Image Courtesy of Lee J Haywood

Did you know that Princess Michael of Kent is a qualified interior designer?

Image Courtesy of Kremlin.ru

Did you know that Prince Andrew was born in the Belgian suite of Buckingham Palace in 1960?

Did you know that Princess Diana was nicknamed the "Bahamas Mama" because she was pictured wearing a bikini on a beach in the Bahamas six months before giving birth?

Did you know that Princess Margaret ended her marriage to Anthony Armstrong-Jones after she alleged he was a secret homosexual?

Image Courtesy of Chris Gulker

Did you know that the Royal family had a dislike for US President Jimmy Carter who they considered too direct?

Did you know that it was George III, the 'Mad Monarch', who purchased Buckingham Palace?

Did you know that the official residence of the Queen Mother was Clarence House?

Image Courtesy of Allan Warren

Did you know that Mark Phillips, (previously married to Princess Anne), was nicknamed 'Fog' because of his apparent lack of intelligence?

Image Courtesy of pochacco20

Did you know that the Queen of England is also the Supreme Governor of the Church of England?

Flag of England and the Church of England

Did you know that Edward VIII abdicated his position of monarch in 1936 after falling in love with the socialite Wallis Simpson?

Image Courtesy of Sporti

Did you know that it was Edward VII, in 1904, who created the "Polar Medal" as this was a great period of Antarctic exploration?

Image Courtesy of British Antarctic Survey

Did you know that Queen Elizabeth II was the first monarch to visit China?

Image Courtesy of www.beijing-travels.com

Did you know that the Koh-i-Noor Diamond is owned by the British Royal family? The Crown Jewel was once the largest known diamond in the world.

Image Courtesy of Chris 73

Did you know that Prince Charles published a children's book in 1980 entitled 'The Old Man of Lochnagar'?

Did you know that the uncle of Prince Philip, Louis Mountbatten, was murdered by the IRA in 1979?

Did you know that Frances Shand Kydd was the name of the mother of Lady Diana Spencer?

Image Courtesy of www.spokeo.com

Did you know that since William the Conqueror (1066), there have been 40 monarchs on the British throne?

Did you know that Tony Blair was the first British Prime Minister to be born within Queen Elizabeth's reign?

Image Courtesy of Chatham House, London

Did you know that Prince William used to own a black Labrador named Widgeon?

Image Courtesy of visualpanic

Did you know that the names of Queen Elizabeth's corgis have included Linnet, Emma, Holly, Willow and Monty?

Image Courtesy of evocateur

Did you know that Queen Victoria only wore black after her husband, Prince Albert, died?

Did you know that Kate Middleton is actually related to George Washington? They are cousins 8 times removed.

Did you also know that Kate is believed to be the first royal to have ever signed a pre-nuptial agreement?

Image Courtesy of Jaqen

Did you know that Princess Diana was was the step-granddaughter of Barbara Cartland? (Famous romantic novelist).

Did you know that Prince William kept a poster of Pamela Anderson on his wall at Eton College? He's only human after all. ☺

That's about it for the royal trivia for now. I'd like to finish this publication with TEN "True or False" questions based on what you've just read. It should help you to really cement the information and to test your memory recall!

....
....

DON'T FORGET TO KEEP YOUR SCORE: THERE'S 1 POINT FOR EACH OF THE FIRST 9 QUESTIONS AND 5 POINTS FOR THE BONUS QUESTION GIVING A TOTAL OF 14 POINTS ....

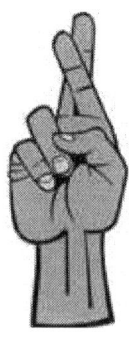

1.

TRUE or FALSE: Prince Philip celebrated not one but two stag nights before his wedding to Queen Elizabeth II.

TRUE.

2.

TRUE or FALSE: Queen Elizabeth described the year 1982 as her 'Annus horribilis' due to the various negative family occurrences.

FALSE

Queen Elizabeth described the year 1992 as her 'Annus horribilis' due to the various negative family occurrences.

3.

TRUE or FALSE: George V had a tattoo of a dragon on his right arm after he visited China.

FALSE

George V had a tattoo of a dragon on his right arm after he visited **JAPAN**.

4.

TRUE or FALSE: No monarch of England has yet held a university degree.

TRUE

5.

TRUE or FALSE: Lady Louise Windsor is the only daughter of Prince Andrew and Sophie.

FALSE

Lady Louise Windsor is the only daughter of Prince EDWARD and Sophie.

6.

TRUE or FALSE: Prince Andrew's golf handicap qualifies him to play at a professional level.

TRUE

7.

TRUE or FALSE: Princess Michael of Kent is a qualified interior designer.

TRUE

8.

TRUE or FALSE: The Queen of England is also the Supreme Governor of the Bank of England.

FALSE

The Queen of England is also the Supreme Governor of the CHURCH of England.

9.

TRUE or FALSE: Harold Wilson was the first British Prime Minister to be born within Queen Elizabeth's reign.

FALSE

TONY BLAIR was the first British Prime Minister to be born within Queen Elizabeth's reign.

10.

BONUS ROUND WORTH 5 POINTS

TRUE or FALSE: Kate is believed to be the first royal to have ever signed a pre-nuptial agreement.

TRUE

Congratulations, you made it to the end!

I sincerely hope you enjoyed my little bear project and that you learnt a thing or two. I certainly did when I was doing the research. Wills & Kate are FAB!

ADD UP YOUR SCORE NOW.

1 point for each of the first 9 correct answers plus 5 points for the bonus round giving a grand total of 14 points.

If you genuinely achieved 14 points then you are indeed a

"ROYAL MASTER".

8 to 13 points proves you are a "ROYAL LEGEND".

4 to 7 points shows you are a "ROYAL ENTHUSIAST".

0 to 3 points shows you are a "ROYAL ADMIRER".

NICE WORK!

Matt.

Thank you once again for choosing this publication. If you enjoyed it then please let me know using the Customer Review Section through Amazon.

If you would like to read more of my work then simply type in my name using the Amazon Search Box and hopefully you'll find something else that "takes your fancy" or go directly to my website printed below.

Until we meet again,

Matthew Harper

www.matthewharper.info

Image Courtesy of Anonymous

Printed in Great Britain
by Amazon